A Riverside Dynasty

By Joan H. Hall

Published by Coyote Hill Press, Camano Island, WA

Layout & Design by Robin S. Hanks

First Edition, 2018

Printed in the United States

ISBN: 978-0-9912641-7-9

Contents

Cornelius Earle Rumsey
Riverside Metropolitan Museum

Foreword

Webster's New World Dictionary defines the word *dynasty* as a succession of rulers or leaders who are members of the same family. Riverside had several early families, the Evans, Gages, and Millers whose members became public leaders during Riverside's formative years and helped advance the community's growth and prosperity.

When Cornelius Earle Rumsey married Mary Elizabeth Marvin in 1874, they remained childless but ultimately became the nucleus of an on-going succession of nieces and nephews, many of whom eventually settled in Riverside.

A large number of relatives in Rumsey's expanding clan became prominent leaders throughout the ensuing years and contributed to the town's history as important members and directors in a variety of civic and philanthropic endeavors.

Although Cornelius Rumsey's residency in Riverside span only ten years, he had the foresight and enthusiasm of enriching his retirement community. He was generous with his energy, opinions, and money. He left a legacy of lasting accomplishment throughout the town and was a strong advocate in the preservation and improvement of Victoria Avenue. Perhaps his greatest contribution to Riverside involved the donation of his vast collection of Indian artifacts that became the nucleus of a city museum.

Even though Cornelius Rumsey appeared aloof and imposing at times, he earned the respect and loyalty of his employees. They trusted his leadership and many of his employees remained in his service for years. He hired workers of all nationalities and treated them fairly and impartially. As a devout member of the Presbyterian Church, he served as an Elder for many years and followed the philosophy of his church.

Although Cornelius and Mary Elizabeth may have retired whereever they desired, they found pleasure and contentment in Riverside. Members of both families were always welcome in the Rumsey's home on Victoria Avenue. Nieces and nephews gravitated to Riverside where they too participated in local social and business affairs.

Today, some hundred years after Cornelius Rumsey passed away, his contributions to Riverside are still enjoyed by new generations. His Indian collection of artifacts located in the Riverside Metropolitan Museum is considered one of the finest in California. Many palm trees gracing Victoria Avenue today were transplanted from his Alta Cresta Ranch. He left a legacy that few could equal and a dynasty of descendents still residing in Riverside, California.

Chapter 1: Cornelius Rumsey & Family

Cornelius Earle Rumsey was laid to rest in New York where he had lived for some thirty years. He was honorably acknowledged in the east and west for his many philanthropic contributions and generosity even though few people were aware of his meager background as a member of an average New York family of six children. Cornelius had only a "common" education yet managed to accumulate great wealth and universal respect. He developed close relationships with family members, a prolific group, with all enjoying his attention and hospitality.

The tall, lean man known as Cornelius Rumsey was born in New York in 1844, one of six children of Thomas O. Rumsey, a New York merchant. He was proud of his family's New England lineage dating back to Revolutionary times. Mother Matilda Earle Rumsey was also a New Yorker and her family had also been in America for decades.

Cornelius E. Rumsey
Riverside Metropolitan Museum

As a young man he maintained a close relationship with his four older sisters and paid less attention to his younger brother Tom. Cornelius found work in a New York City packinghouse where his first work involved physical labor. He eventually graduated to office chores and subsequently gained skills and experience in bookkeeping and secretarial tasks.

In September 1870, his younger sister, twenty-three year old Matilda, married Sylvester Marvin, an enterprising young man who profoundly influenced Cornelius's life. A short time later another sister, Margaret Ann married William Henry Bonnett.

Mary Elizabeth Marvin
Riverside Metropolitan Museum

While working in New York, Cornelius became a member of the First New York Presbyterian Church, known as the Patriots Church, where he participated in religious and social activities. This was the beginning of his life-long devotion to the Presbyterian church. Sylvester and wife, Matilda, belonged to the same church as did a distant cousin, Mary Elizabeth Marvin. Cornelius and Mary

Elizabeth's friendship steadily escalated and they married April 15, 1874 in New York City at the home of her parents. Although this happy marriage did not beget children, the union of these two families resulted in many enduring, happy relationships.

When Cornelius married the charming Mary Elizabeth, he became a member of the proud Marvin clan. His wife was the daughter of Walter Kellogg Marvin, president of the Marvin Safe Company, located in New York since the early 1800s. Azor Marvin, Walter's father, held patents to his inventions for fire-proof and burglar-proof safes. Azor Marvin hired the noted artist Antonio Nicolo to decorate front doors of his custom safes in nautical scenes with boats and sailing vessels; the colorful scenes immediately identified Marvin Safes. The company remained within the family for many years with Mary Elizabeth's brother, Willis, serving as president until the company merged with another in 1882.

During his youth, Sylvester Marvin lived with the Walter Marvin family in New York where he attended school. After his distinguished army service in the Civil War, he settled in Pittsburg, Pennsylvania, and established his own bakery business. During the 1870s, Sylvester's bakery business became very prosperous with a growing clientele and additional stores. He summoned Cornelius to Pittsburg to work for him since his brother-in-law had become a competent, proficient bookkeeper. Cornelius and Mary Elizabeth moved to Pittsburg where they enjoyed a good life for many years. They developed a close relationship with the Marvins who named their sons Walter Rumsey and Earle Rumsey.

Marvin Bakeries produced a variety of items including Oyster Crackers and good old fashion Water Crackers. As the bakery business continued to grow, Sylvester enticed other family members to work in his popular bakeries. Vienna Ovens were installed and special baked bread received an appetizing glossy-like varnish. With so many successful bakeries, Sylvester Marvin soon had more than two hundred fifty employees that included members of both the Marvin and Rumsey clans. Cornelius became the most valuable employee as a trusted secretary and bookkeeper and was compensated with a sizeable interest in the Marvin Baking Company.

Young Edward Mortimer Bonnett, son of Margaret Rumsey and William Bonnett,   began working in the Pittsburg bakeries when additional stores opened during the 1880s. Marvin Bakeries became the largest bakery concern in the nation. Sylvester Marvin was hailed as an industrial mogul, known throughout the United States as the "Edison of Merchandizing." While Marvin Bakeries continued to flourish, both Sylvester and Cornelius increased their assets; by 1889 they both had become wealthy entrepreneurs and partners.

During these prosperous times however, Sylvester and Cornelius experienced sorrowful life changes. Cornelius's father-in-law, Walter Marvin died in 1885 and his widow, Martha Louise, came to live with her daughter and son-in-law. Mrs. Marvin lived a comfortable life with Cornelius and Mary Elizabeth for the next forty years. In 1895, Sylvester's wife Matilda Rumsey, died at the age of forty-eight, a great loss to the entire family. Two years later, Sylvester Marvin married Edith Bonnett, daughter of William and Margaret Rumsey Bonnett.

Throughout the 1880s and 1890s an intense rivalry between bakery companies surfaced with many small companies forced out of business. Bakeries across the nation had begun to consolidate in order to eliminate competition and better control the increasing market for bakery items. During the late 1890s, Sylvester Marvin, then president of United States Biscuit Company, announced the consolidation of three

Edith Bonnett's wedding dress
J. H. Hall Collection

bakery companies involving capital of thirty-five million dollars. When shares were issued, at one hundred dollars each, Sylvester and Cornelius acquired blocks of stock.

On February 4, 1898 the *Boston-Herald* announced that the well-known attorney named Adolphus Green, and his partner, W. H. Moore, had spearheaded the incorporation of the National Biscuit Company. Sylvester Marvin and Cornelius Rumsey were involved in the new corporation that proceeded to purchase some one hundred and fifty bakeries throughout the United States. The National Biscuit Company paid cash for each real estate deed, all assets, bills, plants, and patents. This tremendous consolidation of commercial businesses involved months of planning and diligent work. Cornelius was involved in the acquisition of established bakeries located throughout the states, each with individual laws and regulations.

His valued expertise, and hard work, was acknowledged, however, when he was named secretary-treasurer of the new National Biscuit Company headquartered in Chicago. Cornelius became a large stock holder in the new company as well as a top executive; Sylvester Marvin also purchased blocks of stock in the new company and served on the Board of Directors. The Rumseys, and Martha Louise Marvin, moved to Chicago where Cornelius continued to work long hours dealing with the new company's acquisitions.

As his health began to decline, family members became worried and insisted he see his doctor. He was then informed that his distressing work was taking a toll on his health and his doctor strongly advised a change in his lifestyle. Furthermore, he stated that Chicago winters were adding to his declining poor health and suggested he spend time in a warmer, sunnier climate.

As Cornelius contemplated changing his lifestyle, he accidently encountered an old friend while in Pittsburg. Deloraine Chapman had been a top executive in a Pittsburg insurance company in the 1880s and throughout the years became quite wealthy. He had moved to Riverside, California, where he invested in a citrus grove and became a

The Greatest

Orange Growing District on Earth

Riverside, California

$4000 a Year. "California is wonderful. A man who owns thirty acres is a country gentleman. He does just about work enough to keep himself in good physical condition, and clears from $3000 to $4000 a year. I know one man who makes $3000 a year on ten acres of ground. They press the button and Nature does the rest. The average of intelligence, I should say, is higher than in any other state. It surprises me that everyone who has a little capital has not gone to California to live.

The Most Perfect Type. Thus spoke Chauncey M. Depew after a visit to this state. And he might have added that Riverside is the exponent and example of the highest development in California—material, moral, social, intellectual. Here it is the rule, rather than the exception, for a man to make $3000 a year on ten acres, and very much greater returns are not unusual.

Oranges. A few facts about Riverside that will stand out in your memory are these:

It is the greatest orange-growing district in the world, both as to quantity and quality of its products.

It has two of the most famous avenues in the world, Magnolia and Victoria. Their combined length is twenty miles, mostly through continuous orange groves, within the corporate limits of the city, and aligned with beautiful homes.

Fifty-six Square Miles. The area within the corporate limits of the city is fifty-six square miles, and the colony or district comprises a territory almost twice as large.

There are one hundred and sixty miles of graded streets within the city limits, and the mileage of the city is nearly double that. Eleven miles of the city streets are paved with asphalt and macadam. The natural roads are the finest in all the world —never muddy and very little dust.

Irrigation. Riverside's irrigation systems are among the very finest in arid America. The purity and amplitude of her domestic water supply are not excelled anywhere.

In the city park may be seen the largest and finest collection of cacti in America, if not in the world. This is the testimony of experts and travelers.

Riches. Riverside is the richest city in the world, has the largest per capita income. Yet it has no millionaires and no paupers. There is an equitable distribution of wealth naturally incident to the character of the industries in which the people are engaged, resulting in almost ideal social conditions.

Recreation. In respect of health and pleasure, Riverside stands pre-eminent. It is a place where one can literally live out of doors. The altitude is ideal, ranging from 850 to 1000 feet. The temperature is equable, air dry, rainfall minimum, most sunshine—these are government records. Such conditions make the place a paradise for invalids and sportsmen. There are half a dozen or more golf clubs, several lawn tennis clubs, lacrosse clubs, ball clubs, polo clubs, cricket clubs, gun clubs, wheeling clubs, all occupying foremost rank in the state. The Riverside Country Club has a beautiful home of its own; also the Casa Blanca Lawn Tennis Club. The Rubidoux Club, a gentlemen's social organization, has elegant permanent quarters. The Riverside wheelmen own a fine athletic park. The Woman's Club ranks high among the organizations of its kind.

Social Life. Every phase of social and physical life here reaches the highest development. The general conditions are such as to produce the best type of all round manhood and womanhood, a fact fully attested by the moral and physical standard of the community.

For any Information not contained herein
address

...Riverside Chamber of Commerce...

D. S. Castleman, Secretary   Riverside, California

Riverside Chamber of Commerce Advertisement
J. H. Hall Collection

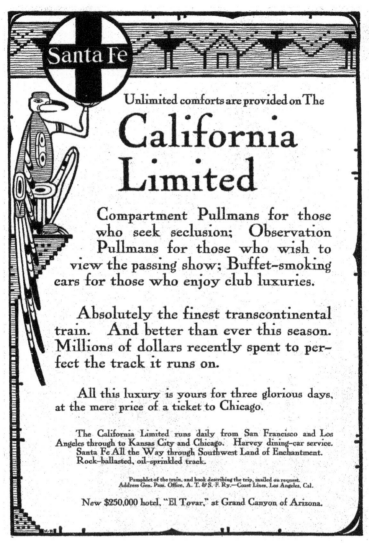

Early Advertisement for the Santa Fe Railroad

successful citrus grower. He said the California climate had improved his health and had given him a most enjoyable life. This unexpected meeting may have been Cornelius

Rumsey's first introduction to a place called Riverside, California.

Serendipity means finding surprising things accidently and when Cornelius told his wife, and mother-in-law, of his visit with Mr. Chapman, the ladies surprised him by knowing all about Riverside. Apparently the Marvin ladies had a distant relative living there named Emma Crosby and they stated she and her husband Chester had lived in Riverside for a number of years.

Cornelius began making inquires about the California community and contacted the *Riverside Daily Press* for information concerning businesses, banks, climate, and advantages of citrus culture. He received a special edition of the newspaper stating "the town was often referred to as the Italy of America." Cornelius took special interest in a statement that read: "An extremely desirable community is being developed known as Arlington Heights with polo grounds, golf courses, and tennis courts all among beautiful terrains of citrus trees."

With encouraging endorsements from family and friends, Cornelius, Mary Elizabeth, and her mother Martha Louisa Marvin, stepped aboard an Overland Train. They occupied private compartments as they traveled west to spend the 1899-1900 winter in Riverside, California.

Chapter 2: Hello Riverside

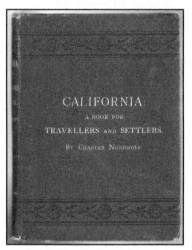

1873 Edition of "California"
by Charles Nordhoff
J. H. Hall Collection

When the easterners arrived at their California resort, the Riverside Glenwood Tavern, it was the start of a new century and the beginning of a new life style for Cornelius Rumsey. "Southern California's healthy climate promised to restore any aliment" so reported Charles Nordhoff, a New York journalist. Rumsey selected the town of Riverside and looked forward to comfortable winter weather and a stress-free environment.

Tourist hotels had sustained a proper "tone" of respectability by 1900 and the Rumseys were pleased with their accommodations. The Glenwood consisted of an elongated wooden building with a series of nearby small cottages featuring glass covered verandas. The Rumseys occupied one of the larger cottages that contained a private bathroom. Meals were served daily in a cheerful dining room located in the nearby main building.

After inspecting their new surroundings, Cornelius, Mary Elizabeth, and her mother, settled down to spend the

The Front of Glenwood Cottages with Guests
Riverside Metropolitan Museum

beginning of a new century in southern California. Frank and Isabella Miller welcomed the Rumsey party to their Glenwood Tavern and introduced them to a number of hotel guests also spending the winter in Riverside. The Rumseys befriended a couple from Minneapolis, Charles Loring and his wife Florence, and they soon were sharing dining facilities in the main building.

Charles Loring and Cornelius Rumsey spent time together sharing their business concerns and accomplishments. Loring claimed he was responsible for the three story office building and opera house located across from the Glenwood and Rumsey shared his connection with the National Biscuit Company. The men took short walks around the grounds of the hotel enjoying the warm sunshine and the tranquility of Riverside, California.

Although the Glenwood lobby was not elaborate, visitors were entertained viewing the display of Frank Miller's Indian collection of baskets, carefully woven rugs, and an unusual wooden Rain Cross symbol. The double cross bars reminded Cornelius of the National Biscuit Company logo with similar cross bars. His personal Indian collection consisted of items from eastern tribes and he found Western Indian artifacts somewhat different and unique.

Trademark used to identify National Biscuit Company products:

Trademark-Logo used by the Glenwood Mission Inn:

Calvary Presbyterian Church
J.H. Hall Collection

Cornelius, Mary Elizabeth, and her mother, attended
Sunday services held in Riverside's Calvary Presbyterian
Church located on the corner of Ninth and Lime streets.
They were warmly welcomed by church members including
Jane and Matthew Gage, charter members of the church.
The Rumseys soon learned Mr. Gage had constructed a ten-
mile long cement irrigation canal in 1888 and had delivered
water to some five-thousand acres being developed as
Arlington Heights. Gage had also built a wooden plank
bridge across the Tequesquite Arroyo in order to reach the
area.

Furthermore, they were told that the main road through
this new development was named for the British Queen,
Victoria, and was designed to resemble Riverside's unique
divided boulevard, Magnolia Avenue. Many cross streets

Matthew Gage
J. H. Hall Collection

along Victoria Avenue had been named for Gage family members; to honor his wife there were two streets, Jane and Gibson, her maiden name.

Rumsey was also informed that Matthew Gage had encountered financial problems in developing Arlington Heights and an English corporation named the Riverside Trust Company Limited purchased Gage's water system and some five thousand acres known as Arlington Heights. Gage had begun planting decorative trees along the curbs of Victoria Avenue and he was now working with, and for, the Trust Company in developing the region.

On the evening of January eighteenth, after eleven o'clock, fire flames swept through the wooden roof of the north wing of the Glenwood Tavern. Frightened guests ran out of their lodgings even though they were not in any immediate danger. A kettle of grease left on the kitchen stove boiled over and started the fire that was quickly extinguished by volunteer firemen. The Rumseys, and other guests, remained safe in their nearby buildings. The following day, hotel guests were given breakfast in nearby restaurants and dinner was served in the Glenwood dining room as usual.

A relaxing routine ensued as hotel guests enjoyed the January climate of sunny days and chilly nights. Hotel guests often remained in the dining room after dinner to exchange greetings and to discuss happenings of the day. One evening when the Rumseys, and Mrs. Marvin. joined the congenial hotel guests, a cheerful gentleman asked if ninety-nine or one hundred years made a century. This was a timely question with the beginning of a new century. Guests expressed their opinions that the new year began with the year one and required a hundred years to make a century.

Glenwood Tavern
J.H. Hall Collection

Another after dinner get-together involved hotel guests discussing the matter of earthquakes since Riverside had experienced several strong shakes just before the turn of the century. Most hotel guests were from the mid-west, or eastern states, and had never experienced such a phenomenon. The Rumseys listened to stories of sudden shocks and strong jolts and Cornelius acknowledged earthquakes to be California's only flaw, so far.

California's Mission Inn--"The Glenwood"

Elegance is not the only attraction of the modern hotel—it's the "home feeling" that counts. When you combine the picturesqueness of the Eighteenth century with the luxury of the Twentieth, and surround them with home comforts and an atmosphere of good cheer, you have described the celebrated GLENWOOD HOTEL, at Riverside.

Proprietor FRANK A. MILLER ∴ ∴ ∴ Illustrated literature on application. ∴ ∴ ∴ Manager MRS. F. W. RICHARDSON

Early Advertisement for The Glenwood Hotel

Chapter 3 : Seeking Information

Emma and Chester Crosby invited the Rumseys, and Mrs. Marvin, to a day of sightseeing around the community of Riverside. Upon their acceptance, Chester hired the finest carriage in the Glenwood Stables operated by Ed Miller, Frank Miller's younger brother. Ed provided his finest rig in his shop complete with a canopy top, spring seats, and a fashionable lap-robe. The Glenwood kitchen staff prepared a special lunch basket and the congenial party took off for a carefree day.

Chester drove the carriage along Main Street towards Fourteenth Street, following the electric streetcar tracks. Along the way, Cornelius observed several substantial business buildings lining Main Street, all with names of their owners, Loring, Hayt, Evans, and Castleman.

Castleman Building
Riverside Metropolitan Museum

As the carriage approached Twelfth and Main Street, commercial enterprises began to give way to several impressive residences. Chester briefly stopped the carriage so his passengers might observe a massive shingled house with a third story tower owned by the Dyer family. The front garden featured sculptured cypress trees surrounding a striking marble water fountain. The Otis Dyer family had moved to Riverside in 1880 in search of a milder climate and Augustus Washington Boggs had built their ten thousand dollar house and their downtown Dyer Bank building.

Chester Crosby continued to Fourteenth Street, then turned west to Brockton Avenue. He explained that Main Street past Fourteenth became Cypress Avenue where a deep ravine known as Tequesquite Arroyo made it difficult for carriages to maneuver the uphill grade. As they continued to Brockton Avenue and Fourteenth Street, Chester commented the ten year old brick high school on the corner had become inadequate and had to be replaced due to the town's increasing population.

Riverside High School
Press-Enterprise Collection

As the sightseers headed up a slight incline known as Brockton Hill, they observed Riverside's Chinatown nearby with its rows of wooden shacks. The Rumseys were informed the compound was occupied by Chinese men who worked as field hands, packinghouse workers, and house servants. Some of the men maintained their own vegetable gardens and peddled fresh produce throughout the town. Cornelius was impressed day laborers were available within the community and employers didn't have to house or feed workers.

Chinatown
J.H. Hall Collection

As the guests reached the top of Brockton Hill, they observed a southern view of flatland with scattered citrus groves and a few modest houses. The carriage turned to connect with Cypress Avenue, past the deep ravine, and proceeded a short distance before stopping in front of Deloraine Chapman's two story frame house. The Chapman family happily greeted their friends and explained they were enlarging

Chapman House
J. H. Hall Collection

their house to ten rooms. A thirteen old citrus grove stood behind their home prompting Cornelius to ask questions concerning the advantages and disadvantages of becoming a citrus grower.

After a pleasant visit, the sightseeing party continued along Cypress to the intersection of Arlington Avenue and the beginning of Magnolia Avenue. The visitors were impressed with the wide, divided road edged in stately palms and majestic magnolia trees. Down the middle of this divided road ran an electric streetcar, a great convenience for residents and tourists.

Chester Crosby stopped the buggy several times along the Avenue to enable his guests to observe numerous private homes belonging to successful businessmen and established families. Most properties were designed with sweeping driveways curving through manicured gardens in front of two or three story mansions. Many owners were former easterners who settled in Riverside seeking a healthier climate.

As the carriage rolled along Magnolia Avenue, Chester realized the ladies were becoming weary. When he came to the end of the divided road, a patch of grass and open space served as a public park. The sightseers walked about to stretch their legs and Cornelius welcomed the exercise for he stood taller than anyone in the group.

The visitors asked a number of questions about Riverside as they relaxed and enjoyed their lunch. They were curious about the summer weather and Chester didn't hesitate to say it was hot in July and August and added whenever possible people headed for the mountains or seashore. The luncheon basket contained a variety of delectable items along with cool drinks and rich desserts.

Magnolia Avenue
Riverside Metropolitan Museum

Chester turned the carriage around to travel north towards town. On this side of Magnolia Avenue there were a series of streets named for former United States Presidents. Between Jackson and Monroe streets a new streetcar park was still under construction. Frank Miller was in charge of the *Riverside & Arlington Railroad Park* that included a zoo, polo fields, and Sunday concerts. This enterprise became known as Chemawa Park, and years later in 1928, Chemawa Junior High School occupied the property. Cornelius asked about the status of a proposed Indian School in Riverside and Chester stated he had been informed that the United States Congress was close to naming Riverside as its location and it appeared it would be built next door to the Streetcar Park.

Magnolia Avenue
J. H. Hall Collection

As the sightseers continued towards town, they passed a large house known as Casa Blanca and continued until they came upon a typical eastern style church known as the

Magnolia Avenue Presbyterian Church. Chester and Emma Crosby were charter members of this church and invited their guests to attend services at their convenience.

The tired party returned to the Glenwood Tavern after a long day of observing many attractive sights in Riverside. The town seemed more and more appealing with its ideal weather, stimulating citizens, and progressive future. However, Cornelius Rumsey was intrigued with the Arlington Heights development and the large commitment of the English group known as the Riverside Trust Company, Limited.

He asked his new friend, Chester Crosby, to escort him about the Arlington Heights area and to share his knowledge of land values and profits, and the true advantages of becoming a citrus grower.

Chapter 4: Arlington Heights

A few days later, Cornelius and Chester set off for Arlington Heights. The two men rode their horses down Fourteenth Street and turned south on Myrtle Avenue and proceeded across the 1891 wooden planked structure known as the Victoria Bridge. It had been rebuilt for electric streetcars to cross, terminating at the foot of Victoria Hill. Cornelius was puzzled why the entire road from Fourteenth Street was not named Victoria Avenue making Arlington Heights easier to locate.

The men proceeded a short distance to the beginning of Victoria Avenue where the road became divided with a strip of land down the middle. Chester Crosby shared the latest gossip concerning Frank Miller's city franchise obtained a few years earlier for a proposed electric streetcar to run

Dedication of Victoria Brige 1891
J. H. Hall Collection

Victoria Avenue 1900
J. H. Hall Collection

from downtown Riverside, across the Victoria Bridge and then down the middle of Victoria Avenue to Van Buren Street. The streetcar line was planned to connect with the existing Magnolia Avenue tracks that would then proceed back to the center of town. City officials anticipated that such a scenic excursion would increase tourism.

Chester added that few residents in the area favored such an undertaking. Home owners were concerned freight trains could use the streetcar tracks for they both ran on the same track gauge. They stated that freight trains traveling down Victoria Avenue would ruin the tranquility of the area and diminish land values. The on-going debate lasted for several years and there were strong objections to having dirty and noisy freight trains running back and forth over Victoria Avenue night and day. Eventually the date of the franchise expired with little regret.

Victoria Avenue 1900
J. H. Hall Collection

As the men meandered along the dirt road, the subject of the Chase family properties unfolded and Cornelius asked about their recent acquisitions involving vast acreage around Riverside. He was informed that Ethan Allen Chase, and three of his sons, had operated a successful nursery business throughout the east before moving to Riverside. The Chase family had opened a local nursery business and was in the process of planting hundreds of acres into thriving citrus groves.

Chester continued talking about the Chases and told Cornelius that Martin, the youngest son, was building a house for his bride just up the road. They inspected the construction of the twelve-room frame house located on the top of a knoll overlooking the countryside. The men returned to Victoria Avenue and proceeded along the road when Chester stopped in front of a citrus grove planted on a slight hill.

The ten acres of Washington Navel Orange trees was owned by Charles Calvin Quinn who was planning to build a family home in downtown Riverside. Chester said the six year old grove was in good condition and appeared to have a sizeable crop. Furthermore, he said the asking price of eighteen thousand dollars was reasonable for the sale would include the crop. Cornelius asked about the size of an acre as they rode around the property several times, sampling an orange or two along the way. Chester explained a Riverside downtown block covered two and a half acres and the Quinn grove was about the size of four city blocks.

As the men continued their inspection trip of Arlington Heights, they came upon construction of another house owned by Robert Henderson, a New York food broker. He had purchased ten acres east of Victoria Avenue and his dark shingled house was said to be the most expensive in Riverside costing more than thirteen thousand dollars. Attractive landscaping with curving roads led to the house to be known as *Edgemont*. The two men continued sight-seeing and came upon a most imposing, tall mansion known as *Raeburn* built in 1895 for William Irving, Matthew Gage's brother-in-law.

Cornelius Rumsey continued to seek additional information concerning future plans for Arlington Heights. Chester informed him the English syndicate had plans to plant thousands of acres into thriving citrus groves with the aid of water from the Gage Canal. The improved land could then sell as income producing home sites and as smart investments. As they made their way along Victoria Avenue, Chester pointed out a grove as a sample of such a sale. He

F. P. HOSP

Florist and Landscape · Architect

Greenhouses

Corner Ninth and
Sedgwick Streets

Riverside, Cal.

Ad in Telephone Books, 1900s
J. H. Hall Collection

said Hamlet Philpot had purchased ten acres of young trees from the Trust Company in 1892 and then built his six room house facing Victoria Avenue. He had become a successful horticulturist and later sold his property for a profit.

A variety of small trees had been planted along the sides of the road. Franz Hosp, a well-known gardener, had been hired by the Trust Company to landscape Victoria Avenue. He planted eucalyptus trees and skinny palm trees that were somewhat foreign to Cornelius Rumsey. As they meandered down the Avenue towards Jane Street, Chester shared more information with his companion.

Matthew Gage's wife Jane owned approximately forty acres of prime land located on Victoria Avenue and Jane Street and she was presently seeking money to assist her husband in his court battles with the Riverside Trust Company. He was again attempting to gain control of the Arlington Heights properties he once owned. It was rumored she was anxious to sell this Victoria Avenue property to help him in his legal battles. When the men reached the property they tethered their horses, and inspected the citrus grove. The two men spent some time discussing the pros and cons of acquiring Jane Gage's land

Within weeks Cornelius Rumsey purchased the C. C. Quinn grove of ten acres for eighteen thousand dollars. The sale included the option to buy the Jane Gage Victoria Avenue property of forty-two acres for thirty-three thousand dollars. He decided Riverside's Arlington Heights would become his retirement home and made his commitment by investing in its future development.

Victoria Avenue 1900
J. H. Hall Collection

A short time later, the Rumseys and Mrs. Marvin returned to their home in Chicago. Cornelius continued working as secretary-treasurer for the National Biscuit Company for the remainder of the year. Before leaving Riverside he had placed a notice in local newspapers announcing: "C. A. Crosby will have charge of Mr. Rumsey's interests here and will occupy the house that will be planned." A profound trust had developed between these two men, one with the wherewithal and the other with knowledgeable experience.

After Cornelius returned to Chicago, he eagerly shared with his relatives his amiable enthusiasm regarding Riverside. A few of his nieces and nephews were concerned about him becoming a farmer, a most unlikely occupation for such an important executive. His usual response indicated the dry climate would improve his health and he didn't plan to dig in the dirt.

The Rumseys discussed the advantages of living in Riverside and decided to make the move, anticipating a stress-free and healthier environment. They were aware of the hot summer months when most people left town, so beneficial to navel oranges but dreadful to humans. Cornelius resumed his duties as secretary-treasurer of the National Biscuit Company then experiencing trouble from anti-trust groups. Good news came in October, however, when Chester Crosby informed Cornelius his Quinn grove was estimated to have seven thousand boxes of good fruit, the finest crop of navels in town.

Chapter 5: A House at 6700 Victoria Ave.

By the first of the year 1901, the Rumseys and Mrs. Marvin, were back at the Glenwood Tavern in Riverside, California. After settling in their apartment, they were warmly greeted by members of the Miller family and hotel guests they had previously befriended. During their absence, the Millers had added a new member to their household. He was a handsome macaw from Ecuador, half wild and half tame, named Joseph. Frank and Isabella Miller had purchased the brilliant colored bird from a sailor in San Diego. Although Joseph's wings had been clipped, he managed to fly wherever he wished. After his daily flights in downtown trees, he would return to the Glenwood near sunset and enter his closet quarters. Hotel guests were entertained by the colorful character and, sometime later, the Millers obtained a companion for him named Napoleon.

While the Rumseys were enjoying their winter at the Glenwood Tavern, Frank Miller introduced Cornelius to a group of impressive gentlemen who often gathered at the hotel. They had recently been successful in obtaining a Federal Indian School to be located in Riverside. Harwood Hall, Superintendent of the existing Perris Indian School, often collaborated with Charles Lummis, a well known historian of southwestern Indians, and Albert K. Smiley, an organizer of the famous Lake Mohonk Indian Conferences held in New York. Cornelius regard these gentlemen, and Frank Miller, reputable civic leaders and graciously joined their efforts to make Riverside's Sherman Indian School the finest Indian School in the west.

Queen Victoria
J. H. Hall Collection

Shortly after the Rumseys arrival in Riverside, news of Queen Victoria's anticipated death appeared in newspapers around the world. On January 24th, the *London Gazette* printed the news of her death in thick, black print. Riversiders honored her memory with combined church services held in Calvary Presbyterian Church. Nearly every pastor in town participated and many Riversiders considered her an accomplished monarch and perfect lady.

Since Cornelius planned to live in Arlington Heights, he suggested to City Trustees that there should be an easier way to find Victoria Avenue from downtown. His recommendation to rename Myrtle Avenue from Fourteenth Street to Victoria Avenue was approved by the Trustees in February 1901; later the Avenue was extended to Eighth Street (University Avenue). The bridge across the Tequesquite Arroyo was reinforced allowing an electric streetcar to cross the Victoria Bridge where it stopped at the end of the line.

On February 1, 1901, forty-two plus acres in the Arlington Heights subdivision, recorded in Jane Gage's name, became the legal property of Cornelius and Mary Elizabeth Rumsey. Due to discrepancies in the original subdivision maps, the transfer of title had been delayed for months. The Rumseys then owned some fifty-two acres in Arlington Heights, most planted in navel orange trees. The long delay in legal ownership had given the couple time to make plans for their future home and other improvements to their surrounding acreage.

The following day, February 2, Cornelius hired Franz Hosp to begin landscaping his Victoria Avenue property for his future home. He hired A. W. Boggs, the well-known architect-contractor, to draw plans for a three-story, eleven room house containing many windows and outdoor

Manager's cottage and barn
Photograph Courtesy of Brad Sackett

Alta Vista Barn
Photograph Courtesy of Brad Sackett

porches to take advantage of healthful fresh air. He also
instructed Boggs to place his house on a slight knoll, facing
Victoria Avenue, in order to capture the view of the distant
San Gabriel Mountains. The Rumsey house was to be fitted
with gas, electricity, and a telephone.

Boggs was also commissioned to build a more modest house
facing Maud Street to be occupied by the Crosby family.
Cornelius concluded his house could wait to be constructed
for he did not plan to return to Riverside until that fall,
after his resignation as secretary-treasurer of the National
Biscuit Company. Boggs was instructed to first construct the
care-taker cottage for Chester Crosby who was overseeing
Rumsey's groves and his presence on the property would
enabled him to better manage the farming operations. After
Boggs completed the Maud Street cottage, he constructed
a two thousand dollar bunk house to be occupied by field

hands; in addition he completed a barn and out-buildings costing more than twenty-five hundred dollars. Later, Boggs built Rumsey's tall, impressive frame house for six thousand dollars and it was christened *Alta Cresta Rancho*.

While making plans for his Victoria Avenue house, Cornelius purchased adjoining property from Frank Miller's brother-in-law, Gustavus O. Newman; the twenty-seven dry acres was purchased for three thousand dollars and an additional three thousand dollars for water rights to the land. In a matter of months Rumsey became owner of seventy-nine acres in Arlington Heights and he was far from finished.

Later that February, the Martin Chase house in Arlington Heights burned to the ground. The nearest water hydrant was located on the north side of the Victoria Bridge and unfortunately the hose was too short to reach the house. Although this was an unfortunate adversity, Martin Chase built a Mission Revival style house of concrete and stucco

Victoria Bridge with Streetcar
J. H. Hall Collection

on the same site. Choice property in Arlington Heights was becoming scarce as visitors and local residents were witnessing many improvements and growth throughout the area.

Two months later, the society page of the *Riverside Daily Press* announced the social event of the year. Mrs. Robert Henderson invited some two hundred and fifty ladies to a reception upon the completion of her house. This exclusive gathering included Riverside's popular and wealthiest matrons and Mary Elizabeth Rumsey and her mother, Mrs. Marvin received invitations.

The castle-like Henderson house sat on a small knoll surrounded by beautiful landscaped gardens. Large plate-glass windows offered magnificent views of the countryside and the spacious rooms were filled with fresh, spring flowers in a variety of colors. Mary Elizabeth Rumsey experienced a sense of friendliness as she mingled with guest and chatted

Henderson House
J. H. Hall Collection

Frank Miller with Joseph & Napoleon
Riverside Metropolitan Museum

with Mrs. Chapman and Mrs. Matthew Gage and other church members.

Shortly after the Henderson reception, the Rumseys returned to Chicago where Cornelius resumed his position as secretary-treasurer of the National Biscuit Company. He planned to retire in the fall and move to Riverside around Thanksgiving time. Consequently on November 27, 1901, the party of Cornelius, Mary Elizabeth, and Mrs. Walter Marvin arrived in Riverside on the Santa Fe Overland Railway. They registered at the Glenwood Tavern where they renewed friendships with the Miller family and hotel guests. Cornelius announced he had just resigned as secretary-treasurer of National Biscuit Company but remained a director on the Board of Trustees. He did not broadcast however, the loss of his ten thousand dollar yearly salary.

Chapter 6: Palm Trees-Orange Trees

Cornelius was informed that during his absence the condition of Victoria Avenue had deteriorated. There was an on-going "misunderstanding" between the City Trustees and the Riverside Trust Company as to which one was responsible for the maintenance of Victoria Avenue. Flowers and foliage planted in the center strip of land had died from lack of water. Cornelius was concerned about this neglect for he had invested considerable funds in the area and had great expectations for Arlington Heights and the future beautification of Victoria Avenue. He was highly pleased to have a Victoria Avenue address and did not wish to see it deteriorate.

Mary and Cornelius Rumsey
J. H. Hall Collection

The Rumsey House
J. H. Hall Collection

Many trees growing in Riverside were foreign to Cornelius. He became especially intrigued with palm trees and consequently had a fifty-three foot high Washingtonia robusta palm moved from a North Orange Street nursery to the middle of his round-a-bout facing his house. Moving the tree, and replanting it, was a huge undertaking but nevertheless the palm thrived and grew taller each year. Eventually it became a local landmark, known as the Rumsey Palm, where colorful flower beds surround its base and bloomed year around. Eventually Mrs. Rumsey posted a sign that read: "Please don't pick the flowers so others may enjoy them."

The Rumseys settled into a comfortable lifestyle whereby Cornelius and Chester Crosby inspected the groves each day and Mary Elizabeth supervised the household, including Chinese houseboys who cooked and cleaned. As

Dosan Ahn Chang-Ho Memorial

Cornelius's health continued to improve, he kept obtaining more property throughout Arlington Heights; apparently it pleased him to transform useless land into attractive citrus groves and potential home sites and the return on his money was notable.

He soon acquired more than two hundred acres in the area and overseeing his properties became a full-time job. Rumsey turned the management of his Riverside enterprises over to Burdette Kellogg Marvin, who had recently moved to Riverside with his wife and children. Burdette, the son of

Willis, and Mary Elizabeth's nephew, was hired to manage Rumsey properties and to oversee the Victoria Avenue household. His duties entailed handling business, and personal matters, for the Rumseys were often out-of-town dealing with National Biscuit Company business.

While Chester Crosby managed citrus grove operations, including planting, irrigating, and harvesting, Cornelius Rumsey was often involved in hiring steady field hands because he felt responsible if they lived on his property. In 1902, an increasing number of citrus workers were Japanese who arrived in November to pick and pack the navel orange crop. One year a religious Korean man, An Chang Ho, worked in the Rumsey groves; many years later he became a spiritual and intellectual leader in a Korean Independent Movement against Japan. He recalled how grateful he was for Cornelius Rumsey's Christian endeavors, and financial aid, in helping Riverside's small Korean community. However, this Asian man was not the only loyal employee at *Alta Cresta Rancho.*

During the early months of 1903, Milford J, Thomas, a black man from Pittsburg, moved to Riverside with his wife, Cornelia. He had worked for both the Rumsey and Marvin families for many years in Pittsburg and was considered a most loyal and competent employee. Cornelius did not hesitate to immediately hire him. Milford drove his horse and buggy from his home on East Tenth Street to Victoria Avenue daily where he was in charge of Mrs. Rumsey's special flower-garden.

A few years after moving to Riverside, Cornelius purchased hundreds of palm tree seeds and had them planted in small

Indian Room in the Rumsey House
J. H. Hall Collection

pots. As the trees grew, they were transplanted into large box-like containers to be eventually planted along roads surrounding *Alta Cresta Rancho*. Some years later, pioneer landscape gardener F. P. Hosp transplanted the remaining palm trees along the borders of Victoria Avenue's middle section.

The Rumseys were enjoying a good life in California and took an interest in learning about western history and the culture of its Native Americans. They began collecting Indian art work, to add to their collection, and didn't hesitate paying top dollar for fine workmanship. As they became known as serious collectors, knowledgeable Indian traders, and tribal leaders, offered Cornelius their finest goods. After purchasing an object, it was tagged to identify the creator and tribe. As their Indian collection continued to increase, a room in their Victoria Avenue home was set aside to store and display their valuable articles.

Although Cornelius Rumsey was becoming one of Riversides largest citrus growers, he had difficulty comprehending how only two navel orange trees could be the nucleus of California's vast orange industry. Again his friend and grove manager, Chester Crosby, informed him that Riversider Luther Tibbets and his wife Eliza, had received two navel orange trees from William Saunders, a former Washington DC neighbor. He worked for the United States Department of Agriculture and when the Tibbets requested free trees in 1873, he mailed them two navel orange trees.

Luther & Eliza Tibbets House
Riverside Metropolitan Museum

Since these were seedless trees it was necessary to remove a bud, or twig, to graft onto a young seedling tree; eventually the seedling tree would become a seedless navel orange tree. The two trees sent by Saunders were planted in the Tibbets garden next to their modest house near Magnolia and Central Avenues. Luther Tibbets, a local character, lost this property due to foreclosure of a loan and in 1899, before the Rumseys arrived in Riverside, Lewis Jacobs, a San Bernardino businessman, took over the Tibbet property. Although the garden received little attention, the two navel orange trees somehow survived. These two trees became somewhat of a legendary dynasty with never ending generations of budded trees.

While Cornelius became involved in Riverside's Chamber of Commerce and the many activities of the Young Mens Christian Association, Mary Elizabeth and her mother joined the pretentious Woman's Club, a fairly new organization dealing with "intellectual improvement, social entertainment, and mutual help."

Ladies in the club were endeavoring to landscape the entrance to the divided portion of Magnolia Avenue beginning at Arlington Avenue. This landscaped road had become a important tourist attraction and entry to the Avenue was in need of attention. The Evans family leased to the City of Riverside, at no cost, a small plot of land at the beginning of the divided road for the relocation of one parent navel orange tree. Cornelius followed the saga of transplanting the tree at his Chamber of Commerce meetings and shared details with his ladies.

Near mid-night in April 1902, Street Superintendent Segar completed moving and planting one tree from Tibbet's former garden to a small plot near the intersection of Magnolia and Arlington Avenues. The future of the second tree became a problem for no one apparently wanted it. A committee of three men, Charles Loring, Albert White, and Cornelius Rumsey went to San Bernardino and acquired the second tree from the estate of Lewis Jacobs. The Riverside Pioneer Historical Society took possession of the second tree due to Frank Miller's offer to plant it near the garden entrance of his new Glenwood Mission Inn Hotel.

In 1902 Frank Miller was chairman of Riverside's Chamber of Commerce whose members invited President Theodore Roosevelt to visit Riverside during his western tour of the United States schedule for 1903. The Chamber of Commerce received the following message in January 1903: "President Roosevelt cannot now determine whether he will be able to accept your invitation." Six months after Roosevelt had been inaugurated as Vice-President, he became President of the United States due to McKinley's assassination. Consequently Theodore Roosevelt's activities were not made public very far in advance.

The years of 1902 and 1903 were filled with an assortment of activities and good times for the Rumseys. In March 1902, the Pinkerton family from Pittsburg were on a western tour of the United States with their grandson,

Car in the Driveway of the Rumsey House
J. H. Hall Collection

Allan. They stopped in Riverside where they visited their former Pittsburg friends, the Cornelius Rumseys. Cornelius escorted the Pinkertons around town and encouraged them to spend a winter in Riverside. Apparently they were not interested and continued their journey without comments. Some twenty years later, however, a mature Allan Pinkerton moved to Riverside where he purchased some forty acres, once owned by Cornelius. On this property, near Victoria and Central Avenues, he built an impressive hilltop house overlooking his two new regulation polo fields.

The Rumseys looked forward to frequent visits from family and friends and their Victoria Avenue home was often the center of much activity. To keep his visitors entertained, Cornelius would often disclose the sporting events then taking place in Riverside. There were frequent activities at the Casa Blanca Tennis Club, week-end polo matches, and year around golf matches at the Pachappa Golf Club. The golf course, located south of Pachappa Mountain, was a dirt, nine hole course.

Chapter 7: The Good Life

While Cornelius Rumsey was engaged in acquiring more acreage to enlarge his citrus holdings in Arlington Heights, major developments were taking place in downtown Riverside. In May 1902, the Glenwood Tavern closed and was replaced with a two-hundred seventy-five room, modern tourist hotel. Across the street from the hotel, a Carnegie Free Library had been constructed in a Mission Revival style of architecture. These major projects, along with other buildings, undoubtedly increased Riverside's esteem and popularity.

President Theodore Roosevelt eventually accepted Riverside's invitation to visit the City during his 1903 western tour. He also accepted Frank Miller's invitation to spend the night in his new Glenwood Mission Inn. City officials, and local organizations, instantly began planning numerous activities and ceremonial functions.

Victoria Avenue Expansive View
J. H. Hall Collection

Cornelius Rumsey was a member of the Chamber of Commerce in 1903 and served on the Board of Directors. He shared his ideas concerning the upcoming visit of the President of the United States and suggested he could plant a commemorative palm tree at the head of Victoria Avenue in memory of Queen Victoria. After city officials agreed to his proposal, members of the Riverside Historical Society accepted Frank Miller's offer to replant the remaining parent navel orange tree in the garden of his new Glenwood Mission Inn Hotel while the President was in town. Some weeks later, city officials received the President's message that he would be honored to participate in both ceremonial tree events.

When President Roosevelt traveled west in May 1903, his entourage stopped to view the wonders of Grand Canyon. Charles Lummis joined the Presidential Party there and escorted dignitaries about the historic sites and joined the railroad party to California. Lummis and Roosevelt had attended Harvard University at the same time and both gentlemen enjoyed the great outdoors and beauties of nature.

Before the Presidential party reached Redlands, Federal Agents made a thorough search of the Glenwood Mission Inn, and all areas to be occupied by President Roosevelt. Since it was but twenty months since President McKinley had been assassinated, and Vice President Roosevelt became President, great caution prevailed.

After the President's train left Redlands, it traveled through downtown Riverside and stopped at Pachappa Station in Arlington Heights. There, eleven waiting carriages were

Teddy Roosevelt Planting The Orange Tree at The Mission Inn

lavishly decorated in pink roses and the many horses wore collars of yellow roses. The President's carriage had an open hood in order for him to enjoy the sights and for the general public to enjoy seeing him. The caravan traveled up Jane Street to Victoria Avenue and entered Cornelius Rumsey's property. The line of rose covered carriages slowly encircled the beautifully landscaped garden in front of the stately three-storied house. There, each carriage briefly stopped to receive a fancy basket of navel oranges from Rumsey's grove.

Roosevelt Palm and Martin Chase House
J. H. Hall Collection

The Presidential procession then headed north along Victoria Avenue, slowly moving in order for the visitors to enjoy the scenery of thriving citrus groves. When the caravan reached the end of the divided road, actually the beginning of Victoria Avenue, dignitaries gathered around a small dirt area and formally dedicated a fifty-five foot high Washingtonia robusta palm tree in memory of Queen Victoria. Throughout the years, however, this tree became known as the Roosevelt Palm.

During the dedication ceremony of planting the tree, Cornelius was busy making sure every detail was in place. He did not notice until sometime later that a sizeable diamond was missing from his ring. It apparently came loose during the replanting and later search parties attempted to locate the stone unsuccessfully.

While the President was housed in the most deluxe suite in the Glenwood Mission Inn, Charles Lummis and other members in the Presidential party received rooms throughout the hotel. On the evening of May 7, four hundred people, including the Rumseys, attended an elaborate banquet honoring President Roosevelt. Before the President departed the following morning, he participated in replanting the second parent navel orange tree sent to Luther and Eliza Tibbets.

In formal attire, the President joined a gathering in the courtyard of the Glenwood Mission Inn where President John North of the Historical Society stated:"The two trees, of which this is one, were brought from Bahia, Brazil and sent to Riverside by the Agricultural Department at Washington in 1874. From these two tress, by process of budding into seedling stock, all of the navel orange trees in California have sprung."

The President then shoveled a small amount of dirt over the roots of the tree, said a few words, and was ready to depart. Overhead, near the roof of the hotel, flew the United States Presidential Flag with thirteen stars on a blue field with arrow and olive branches. As carriages carrying the Presidential Party, including Charles Lummis, headed for the train depot, hotel chimes played *Fair Harvard* as a farewell tribute to President Theodore Roosevelt.

During Cornelius Rumsey's involvement with the President's visit, a young couple from London, England, Hugh and Adelaine Newton, purchased fifty-two acres near Madison Street and Victoria Avenue, not far from *Alta Cresta Rancho*. Hugh Newton's father was chairman of the Riverside Trust Company, and the major stockholder of the organization.

 The young couple built a one-story, marble brick house on the Madison Street hill overlooking their navel orange grove. This eccentric marble residence became locally known as Newton Place. Hugh and Adelaine befriended their neighbors, including members of the Rumsey household.

After Hugh's father, T. H. G. Newton, paid an unexpected visit to his son, and to check on the operations of the Riverside Trust Company, the young couple silently, and quickly returned to England. Mr. Newton sold all his Riverside Trust Company stock and refuse to have any dealings with the company. Whatever transpired, or whatever he may have uncovered, remains a mystery. Local speculations concerning the Riverside Trust Company management remained a timeless, unanswered subject.

TAHOE TAVERN
ON THE SHORE OF LAKE TAHOE

The Most Picturesque Mountain Lake in America

Accommodates 350 Guests

New Annex   New Casino

Fifteen miles by rail from Truckee, Cal. Stop-overs permitted on Overland Railroad and Pullman tickets

Excellent trout fishing, boating, driving, mountain climbing, etc.

ADDRESS
MRS. ALICE RICHARDSON, MANAGER, TAHOE, CALIFORNIA

Advertisement for Tahoe Tavern
J.H. Hall Collection

When the new Glenwood Mission Inn opened for business in January 1903, it quickly became a renown tourist destination. The three-story building contained nearly three hundred hotel and public rooms. However, after five months of operation, the hotel closed for the summer. It was customary for Riverside establishments to curtail business during July, August, and September due to the intense heat. Hotel employee were dismissed, except for a skeleton crew as several hotel rooms remained available for the occasional traveler.

Frank Miller's sister, Alice, and her husband Frank Richardson, had managed the Glenwood for a number of years and continued to be in charge of the new Mission Inn Hotel. Nevertheless, they made arrangements to manage the Tahoe Tavern in Nevada during the summer months of 1903 and took two key employees from the Riverside hotel to assist them. The Richardsons encouraged Cornelius and Mary Elizabeth Rumsey to spend the summer at Tahoe Tavern where they could enjoy the cool mountain air. The Rumseys, and Mrs. Marvin, spent that summer, and many more, at the Tahoe Tavern where they not only enjoyed the mountain atmosphere but were also able to pursue their interest in authentic Native American art items. They became well-known among Indian traders in Nevada. Arizona, and New Mexico, serious collectors with money and little consideration as to price when it came to acquiring authentic works of art.

During one of his occasional collecting tours, he had the opportunity to purchase eight hundred specimens of unique pottery gathered in a secluded Arizona cave. Cornelius

Rumsey bought the entire collection and presented the priceless, rare collection to the Anthropology Department of the University of California. The 1904 gift was given in memory of Anton Roma, a close friend of both the Rumsey and Marvin families. Hearst newspapers publicized his contribution and Mrs. Randolph Hearst commented, "It is hoped other Californians would follow Mr. Rumsey's example on providing means for increasing the University collection." Cornelius was now a celebrated Californian.

He had also become a well-known, likeable Riversider where people readily recognized the gentleman when he drove his spiffy White Steamer auto around town. The tall, lean man, always smartly attired, made a good impression in any group and supported and served on a number of local boards including the Chamber of Commerce, Young Men's Association, his Presbyterian Church, and the Victoria Avenue Improvement Association. He was indeed enjoying the good life.

Chapter 8: Relatives and Neighbors

The Rumseys experienced an above average rainfall during one of their early winters in Riverside with periodic rainstorms measuring thirteen inches of rain. Dirt roads, occasionally oiled by the Street Department, developed large holes and ruts from the heavy rain causing residents to complain. Cornelius soon learned paving entailed crushing small stones or gravel, with tar or asphalt, into a mixture that was used to fill in holes. After the City owned rock quarry ran out of gravel, Trustees started getting gravel from small hills surrounding Victoria Avenue. When Cornelius realized dynamiting activities were not far from his Victoria Avenue home, he took action to stop the operation.

First, Cornelius purchased four unimproved acres used by the Pachappa Golf Club as a nine-hole golf course. This rent free property, located south of Pachappa Hill along Central Avenue, may have been considered a source of available gravel. Rumsey's acquisition forced the City, and local golfers, to seek new locations for their diverse enterprises. Consequently, golfers decided to secure permanent grounds and a group of influential men incorporated the Victoria Club in 1903. Rumsey became a charter member subscribing five shares at five hundred dollars each.

The Church Quarry, owned by Richard and Berta Church, was located east of Victoria Avenue, beyond the Pachappa Golf course. The property included thirteen acres of rock and Cornelius did not hesitate to purchase the quarry, planning to sell it to the City. He reasoned this would stop the blasting in the hills surrounding Victoria Avenue. However, the City was not interested in Cornelius's proposal since they had obtained another source of gravel and cease operations near his home. Some years after Cornelius's death, Mary Elizabeth Rumsey sold the Church Quarry to the City of Riverside at a loss.

City Trustees continued to defer action concerning the proposed electric streetcar route projected to run down the middle section of Victoria Avenue. Residents had opposed this proposition for several years. Finally, in August 1906, the franchise for the electric line expired; no one complained nor seemed to notice the end of the proposed scenic route down Victoria Avenue. However, the Victoria Avenue Electric Streetcar continued operations from downtown, traveling across the Victoria Bridge, and ending near the clubhouse entrance to the posh Victoria Clubhouse.

Victoria Clubhouse
J. H. Hall Collection

Another Arlington Heights landmark came to life when a road around Rumsey's grove, purchased from Mr. Quinn in 1900, was professionally landscaped. A variety of trees and flowering scrubs were planted along the roads surrounding the diminishing citrus grove. Most of this property had become an exclusive residential area with a private road known as Rumsey Drive or Rumsey Hill. Although many Riversiders believed Cornelius and his wife lived on Rumsey Drive, it is doubtful he would ever relinquish his Victoria Avenue address.

Alta Cresta Rancho continued to be a happy destination for the Rumsey's nieces and nephews and their increasing families. Edward Bonnett, his wife, and four children were frequent visitors and the William Henry Bonnett family of four children often stayed with their Aunt and Uncle in Riverside. Former eastern neighbors and acquaintances were always welcomed and consequently Doctor William Fundenburg of Pittsburg arrived in Riverside in 1907 to visit his friend, Cornelius Rumsey. The men had worked together at a Pittsburg hospital where Rumsey was a major fundraiser and Fundenburg owned a large eye-glass company.

The wealthy Doctor was intrigued with Riverside and in no time decided to make Arlington Heights his winter home. He purchased the Hugh Newton property on Madison Street that included a one-story, six-room hilltop house overlooking the adjoining citrus grove. He paid fifty-seven thousand dollars for the grove and house and hired a highly regarded architect, Franklin P. Burnham, to add a second story of five bedrooms. The enlargement and remodeling of the house cost an additional five thousand dollars.

That winter, the Fundenburgs moved into their hilltop home. Cornelius offered to take visiting relatives of the

Fundenburgs on a sightseeing trip in his big White Stanley Steamer automobile. The guests were taken down Victoria Avenue and were fascinated by the vast acreage devoted to Washington navel orange trees. Upon returning to the Fundenburg house, Cornelius encountered a pile of lumber stacked on the hillside driveway. When he attempted to back up, one wheel slipped over the embankment and the car flipped over, landing on its top.

The passengers were pinned inside the car and aid came quickly after hearing the yelling for help. Occupants were taken to the Fundenburg house where doctors soon arrived. Cornelius had broken three ribs plus his collarbone. A twelve-year old boy had a broken arm and other passengers suffered bruises and cuts, however, all survived the unfortunate ordeal.

Fundenburg House
J. H. Hall Collection

Cornelius Rumsey kept well informed concerning new and different developments in the citrus business. Chester

Crosby had created a typical citrus packing shed in the grove adjacent to the Rumsey house. Here the fruit was picked, washed, and packed and then hauled to the railroad station to be transported to eastern markets. Cooperative packinghouses entailed numerous growers who pooled their fruit, and farming equipment, in an effort to reduce expenses. Rumsey packed his own fruit and instigated his own rules and regulations. Each picker and packer received a number to identify poor performers.

Citrus growers had been losing money since 1900 due to decay of their boxed fruit and they could not find a solution. Consequently, the United States Department of Agriculture

Alta Cresta Groves Crate Label
J. H. Hall Collection

sent an expert horticulturist to Riverside named G. Harold Powell, to investigate. Eventually Dr. Powell discovered that careless and rough handling of the fruit, both in picking and packing, injured fruit causing quicker decay. This simple solution saved hundreds of dollars for growers. Cornelius Rumsey was so impressed with Powell he placed a special placard on his packinghouse at Pachappa Station: "This building dedicated to G. Harold Powell, and associates, to the careful handling of fruit." Some years later, this packinghouse burned to the ground, a common occurrence due to cheap wooden buildings harboring vast amounts of wax.

Chapter 9: Murder on Victoria Avenue

Cornelius and Mary Elizabeth Rumsey become well-known throughout Riverside due to their generosity, Christian endeavors, and leadership qualities. Burdette Marvin had taken over their business concerns, and household maintenance, giving the couple freedom to pursue special interests. Their capable Japanese houseboy, William Shimizu, cooked and cleaned and became their most reliable servant for a number of years. However in 1907, the peaceful tranquility at 6700 Victoria Avenue changed and became the site of a premeditated murder, and a carefully planned suicide.

When thirty-five year old Shimizu began working for the Rumseys in 1904, he became devoted to the family, and especially dedicated to Mary Elizabeth. He was a hard worker, completely trustworthy, and was allowed sleeping quarters in the large house. Several years later Frank Kojima, a young Japanese man, was hired as a butler. William took an instant dislike to the younger man who was also allowed to live in the Rumsey house that William considered his own domain.

Shimizu was jealous of everyone who received attention from either of the Rumseys and his hostile attitude extended to family members. Cornelius's nephew Edward Bonnett often stayed at *Alta Cresta Rancho* to visit his uncle for the two men shared many common interests having worked together in Sylvester Marvin's early Pittsburg bakeries. As Shimizi's jealous resentments seemingly increased, he

began to believe Mrs. Rumsey was paying too much attention to the younger butler and he threatened to quit several times. His moody behavior and sudden emotional outburst had everyone worried.

On April 16, 1907, William Shimizi asked, and received, permission to take the day off for matters of personal business. He climbed on his nickel-plated bicycle and pedaled downtown to Main Street where he first stopped at the Riverside Cycle and Sporting Goods Store. There he bought a .38 caliber pistol, paying for it with a fifty-dollar bill, one of several in his pocket. He then proceeded to Rouse's Department Store where salesman Fred Younglove waited on him.

William purchased a new suit of underwear, a short black coat, black pants, a white vest, and a shiny pair of patent leather shoes. Fred Younglove, in a cheerful manner, asked his customer if he was planning to get married in such a formal outfit. William's sullen, mysterious response indicated something unexpected might happen as he left the store in a hurry. His final errand took him to the post office where he sent a one hundred fifty dollar check, by register mail, to an unknown person in Japan.

Cyclery Shop in Riverside
J. H. Hall Collection

While William Shimizu was gone from the house, the Rumseys grasped the opportunity to find a cause for William's strange behavior. Mary Elizabeth phoned her doctor and explained in detail the strange behavior of her servant and asked advice how to best handle the situation. In the meantime, Cornelius, and his visiting nephew Edward Bonnett, held a secret meeting with a few of William's Japanese friends in an effort to find the cause of his unhappiness. As the men gathered in Rumsey's dining room, William Shimizi returned home to discover the secret meeting discussing his well-being. He became enraged to find these men talking about him behind his back and told his employer he was leaving for good the next day. He stormed up the back steps to his room and slammed the door.

That evening Frank Kojima, the butler, prepared and served the evening meal. After dinner the family gathered in the front parlor to discuss William's behavior and how they could best help him. While Frank cleaned the table and washed the dishes, William remained in his room and silently planned his Japanese ceremonial rites of revenge.

First, he carefully bathed himself and then meticulously began putting on his new clothes, priming and fussing with each garment until he was completely satisfied with his appearance. Then he silently left his room and went down the back stairs leading to the kitchen. There he hid behind the swinging door, connecting the dining room and kitchen, and waited for the right moment to end Frank Kojima's life. He believed Mrs. Rumsey favored Frank, paying him too much attention, and had stopped relying on his management of the household.

William waited for the right moment to use his gun and when it came, his first shot went wild and missed its mark. More determined than ever, William boldly pointed the gun at Frank's heart and killed him. The force of the bullet propelled Frank into the dining room where he came to rest on the thick carpet. William then ran out the back door, climbed on his bike and disappeared into the night.

Cornelius Rumsey phoned Sheriff Frank Wilson to report the shooting of his butler and the disappearance of his houseboy. It was 8:30 when Sheriff Frank Wilson, and his deputies, arrived at the Rumsey house where they found Frank Kojima sprawled on the dining room floor in pools of blood. They were informed of William Shimizu's jealous attitude and profound dislike of Frank. Members of the posse decided it was too dark to search for the missing Japanese man and postponed their investigation until daylight. Sheriff Wilson did however send a request to surrounding communities to arrest Shimizu on sight. He was described as a Japanese male, about forty years old, with a gold tooth on his right upper jaw.

Early the next morning a neighbor of the Rumsey's noticed an abandoned bicycle near his house and discovered a dead man slumped beneath a tree. William Shimizu, dressed in his new clothes, had shot himself in the stomach. He had performed an ancient Japanese suicide ritual known as "hara-kiri." The Rumseys treated the deaths of William Shimizu and Frank Kojima with equal respect. They held double funeral service for the two Japanese men who were laid to rest next to each other in Olivewood Cemetery.

During the period of William Shimizu's employment, Mary Elizabeth and Cornelius followed the sage of the Kellogg brothers who were making news in newspapers across the nation. Mary Elizabeth's father, and Mrs. Marvin's deceased husband, had a vague relationship with the Kellogg family and thus kept abreast of the infighting between Dr. John Kellogg and his brother William, both Seventh Day Adventist.

Dr. John Kellogg supervised the Battle Creek Sanitarian in Michigan where only vegetarian meals were served. The brothers believed spicy foods increased passions and masturbation. They recommended a healthy lifestyle with a diet of whole grains, low fat, and lots of fresh air and exercise. Their dietetics became known as sanitarium health foods. The

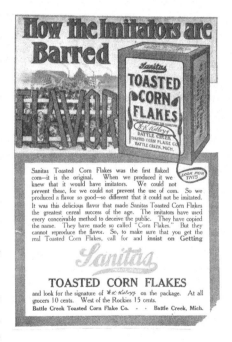

brothers experimented modifying cooked wheat flakes and accidently discovered a good mixture, later marketed as corn flakes.

Several years earlier, on October 9, 1905, the *Riverside Daily Press* announced that the nearby Loma Linda Hotel had been purchased for sanitarian purposes. It was announced that the Loma Linda Sanitarian employed only graduate nurses from the Battle Creek training school. The Battle Creek method of treatment had obtained a reputable name.

A short time later, the brothers began fighting over control of the company they had started together and their legal battles lasted for years. Eventually Kellogg's Corn Flakes became a house-hold item and could be found in the *Alta Cresta Rancho* kitchen shelves. Also a tray of homegrown oranges was usually available in the Rumsey kitchen.

Oranges from the parent navel orange tree planted in the Glenwood Mission Inn garden in 1903 were harvested for several years and shipped to President Theodore Roosevelt. This custom was well received by the President and Riverside received special recognition for producing excellent navel oranges.

Chapter 10: Passing of Rumsey

During his years in California, Cornelius Rumsey became aware of the many problems involving Native Americans and their need for better living conditions and stronger laws. Doctor David Starr Jordon, president of Stanford University, and Frank Miller organized a state-wide conference held at the Mission Inn in April 1908 to discuss Indian affairs and their urgent needs. It was a diverse group involving tribal chiefs, distinguished educators, and church representatives. The session was called to order by Cornelius Rumsey who introduced important leaders and organizers attending the unusual conference. Rumsey had become an imposing

1908 Mission Indian Conference at the Mission Inn
Riverside Metropolitan Museum

notable leader and a highly respected gentleman well versed in Indian culture. The two-day gathering ended with several possible resolutions and many congenial friendships.

In 1909, President William Howard Taft visited Riverside where he was warmly welcomed and given a whirlwind tour of the town. His entourage was taken to the top of Mount Rubidoux, around downtown, and then down scenic Victoria Avenue. At Jane Street the parade of cars stopped in front of Cornelius Rumsey's home where President Taft enjoyed the colorful gardens and observed a second floor flagpole holding a large American flag. After visiting Sherman Institute, the President returned to the Mission Inn for an elaborate banquet in his honor. While at the hotel, he was seated in an oversized chair that had been created for the hefty dignitary. President Taft spent five hours in what he called "the City Beautiful" and then boarded his Presidential train waiting on Market Street.

Victoria Avenue continued to have maintenance problems as City Trustees and property owners could not agree as to planting, watering, and supervision. Many Victoria Avenue property owners, including Rumsey, paid their gardeners, or field hands, to irrigate vegetation within the center strip when city workers failed to do so. Cornelius Rumsey provided hundreds of palm trees, grown in tubs on his ranch, that were transplanted along the median borders of the Avenue. Victoria Avenue received a great deal of attention from Rumsey, a fact not generally publicized. In April 1910, a sign appeared near the Roosevelt palm tree that read: "Picking flowers or shrubs on Victoria Avenue prohibited by law, under control of Board of Park Commissioners."

27th President of the
United States, 1909-1913

TAFT, WILLIAM HOWARD (1857-1930)

President William Howard Taft

As an avid supporter of the YMCA, Cornelius Rumsey served on the Board of Directors when the organization had the opportunity in 1906 to purchase land for a much needed newer facility. With political and financial support from Rumsey, the building site was obtained and a building fund was instigated. Three years later, the seventy-thousand dollar, three-story structure was completed.

On November 5,1909, the President of the YMCA Board of Directors, Cornelius E. Rumsey, presided over opening ceremonies of the long awaited facility. Large crowds inspected the well-equipped gym, first floor meeting rooms, and second floor rental rooms for young men. The open-house festivities lasted a week and Cornelius, and his fellow directors, received high praise for the new facility.

A year later Andrew Carnegie, a wealthy steel tycoon and generous philanthropist, arrived in Riverside aboard his

Sherman Institute
Riverside Metropolitan Museum

private deluxe train. The self-made man lived in Pittsburgh the same time Cornelius resided there and they may have been acquainted. Nevertheless, Carnegie and his fellow travelers filled eleven Riverside automobiles that conveyed them down Magnolia Avenue to the Carnegie financed Arlington Branch Library. On route, the party briefly stopped at Sherman Institute and observed the campus with attractive Mission-style buildings.

The dignitaries arrived in the small community of Arlington where Carnegie, and his party, inspected the year old City branch library financed by the Andrew Carnegie Foundation. Riverside Fire Station Number 2 occupied a room attached to the back of the building. After a quick tour, the caravan proceeded to Jane Street and Victoria Avenue where cars pulled into Cornelius Rumsey's driveway edged in beautiful scrubby and foliage.

As the cars stopped in front of the impressive three story house, the tourists observed rows of tall palm trees lining the roads around Rumsey's citrus grove. They were delighted when seven-year-old Sylvester Marvin, Cornelius's grand nephew, gave each car a basket of *Alta Cresta Rancho* fruit and served willing occupants glasses of fruit juice. The entourage long remembered the Cornelius Rumsey house and the little boy with oranges and juice.

The Carnegie party then proceeded down Victoria Avenue, pass the Victoria Palm, and headed for downtown Riverside. The spectators walked through the lobby of the Mission Inn and headed across Orange Street to the Carnegie Library. There Andrew Carnegie briefly addressed the small crowd from the library steps and then he and his party boarded their waiting trains. Carnegie and his companions continued

Carnegie Library
J. H. Hall Collection

their goodwill tour visiting other Carnegie financed libraries throughout California.

It had been a busy year for sixty-six year old Cornelius with his many business dealings, his ownership of some four hundred acres of citrus, his continuing interest in adding to his Indian collection, and his volunteer involvement in city activities. Towards the end of 1910, Cornelius and Mary Elizabeth Rumsey took a vacation to relax and to temporarily escape all responsibilities. Upon their return to Riverside, Cornelius seemed tired and appeared to have suffered some slight paralysis. However, he was quite amused during the holidays when a local newspaper printed this advertisement, "Give your son or daughter a Victoria lot for Christmas -five dollars down - one dollar a week -no interest -south of the Victoria Club." Only catch, no mention of the total price.

After the Christmas holidays, Cornelius Rumsey checked into the Loma Linda Sanitarian for continued rest and observation. His health continued to deteriorate and his nephews Edward Bonnett and Sylvester Marvin, arrived at *Alta Cresta Rancho* to visit their favorite uncle and to assist Mary Elizabeth.

As the weeks passed, there was little improvement in his declining condition. In February a vein in his brain burst and Cornelius became unconscious. Although his death was emanate, he lingered on for a week, passing away in his sleep on Saturday February 25, 1911.

Chapter 11: Alta Cresta Rancho

Funeral services for Cornelius Earle Rumsey took place in the Calvary Presbyterian Church at three-thirty on the afternoon of February 28, 1911. The Normandy style building appeared massive with its tall corner tower and heavy plate-glass doors. More than five hundred friends, relatives, and admirers filled the pews and addition seating became necessary. Many of his twenty-two nieces and nephews were present. Rumsey's newspaper obituary stated: "Friends will kindly omit flowers."

Aging Chester Crosby was honored to be a pallbearer and accompanied members of the Marvin and Bonnett families in caring for the casket. Cornelius was properly eulogized for his many public services and his devotion to Riverside. The afternoon sun came streaming through the magnificent cut-glass windows and added a bright moment to an otherwise sad occasion. His interment took place later, in Woodlawn Cemetery, New York.

A month or so went by before the Riverside law firm of Purington & Adair requested a copy of Cornelius Rumsey's last will in order to begin probate proceedings. Mary Elizabeth Rumsey searched her husband's desk, and his many files, and could not locate his will. Months went by, and almost a year passed when on January 17, 1912, the elusive holographic will surfaced. It was discovered in an old oak desk stored in the ranch barn. Surplus furniture had concealed the desk and no one had considered the barn a depository for such an important legal document.

His will, dated March 6, 1885, left his entire estate, estimated in excess of one hundred thousand dollars to Mary Elizabeth. One provision stated that her will include his relatives and another provision establish two permanent endowments of one thousand dollars each for the YMCA and Sherman Institute, Riverside's Indian school. When Mary Elizabeth obtained letters of administrator, she distributed forty thousand dollars among Cornelius's relatives.

Mary Elizabeth and her mother, Martha Marvin, remained in the large house on Victoria Avenue. Burdette Marvin continued to manage household expenditures and bills associated with *Alta Cresta Rancho*. Chester Crosby supervised the grove properties then consisting of more than four hundred acres. After Rumsey's death, Crosby was put in charge of an estate sale involving a few insignificant items including outdated farm equipment, farm animals named Fanny and Jenny, and a 1906 White Steamer automobile. One of Mary Elizabeth's first purchases after Cornelius's death, was a seven passenger motor car; she may have retained a chauffeur but it is likely she learned to drive.

Forty-six year old Edward Mortimer Bonnett, his wife Lucy and their four children, moved to Riverside after Cornelius Rumsey's death in 1911. They settled in downtown Riverside where their children could easily attend both grammar and high school. Graduates of Riverside High School were automatically admitted to higher institutions without examinations due to Riverside's excellent education system. Some years later, several generations of Bonnetts attended

Woman's Club
J. H. Hall Collection

Stanford where they encountered their future wives and or
husbands.

Mary Elizabeth filled her days with a variety of activities
and volunteer projects. Both she and her mother became
active participants of the Woman's Club where they enjoyed
a compatible social life. Mary Elizabeth also took over the
management of the Rumsey real estate interests. Even
though she had no worries concerning money, it wasn't
long after Cornelius's death she began selling parcels of
land, improved and otherwise.

One of her early transactions involved the Church quarry,
land Cornelius had purchased in order to stop the city from
blasting the hills around Victoria Avenue. Mary Elizabeth
Rumsey deeded to the city eleven acres of the Church Quarry
for the sum of five thousand dollars. And this was just the
beginning. For the next fifteen years, Mary Elizabeth sold

considerable property, improved and otherwise, throughout the Victoria Heights area.

In February 1920, Burdette Marvin resigned as supervisor of *Alta Cresta Rancho* and manager of Mary Rumsey's domestic expenditures. He had taken care of the financial needs of Rumsey's groves for nineteen years and the time had come when he wished to pursue his own interests. Some years earlier, Burdette had invested in a desert date farm and it had developed into a growing business known as the Marvin Date Company. He was also involved in the Red Mountain Fruit Company and had interests in other agricultural enterprises. Some years later, Burdette Marvin became a well-known writer, and critic, with his commentaries appearing in local newspapers.

Chester Crosby was in his late seventies when he retired in the 1920s. Milford Thomas and Charlie Yamaguchi continued working for Rumsey relatives throughout the 1930s and 1940s.

One of Mary Elizabeth's most memorable sales transactions took place in 1922 when Colonel Allan Pinkerton decided to make Riverside his new winter home. He had spent several winters in Colorado Springs after serving in the Intelligence Corps during World War 1 where he encountered poison gas causing him to become a semi-invalid. Allan Pinkerton recalled his 1902 visit to Riverside with his grandparents when they visited their friends, the Rumseys. He was not pleased with winters in Colorado Springs and consequently decided to spend the 1919 winter at the Mission Inn in Riverside, California.

He favored southern California climate and was also attracted to the city's active interest in the game of polo. A Riverside Polo Club had organized in 1892 due to the influx of English gentlemen connected with the new Riverside Trust Company. Throughout the years, several polo fields had been developed and the game became a popular spectator sport. Although Allan Pinkerton was not able to participate in sporting activities, he had once been an avid horseman and excellent polo player; his interest and enthusiasm for polo never ceased.

The millionaire spent three winters in Riverside. He then decided the town was where he would build his winter residence and planned to renew interest in local polo matches. In January 1922, Mary Elizabeth Rumsey sold Allan Pinkerton forty-six acres of citrus property near

Pinkerton House
J. H. Hall Collection

Victoria Avenue
Riverside Metropolitan Museum

the corner of Central and Victoria Avenue, across the road from Rumsey's Quinn grove, then known as Rumsey Hill. Pinkerton's purchase was considered prime property since it was located on two major thoroughfares.

Pinkerton built a twenty-room, hilltop house for twenty thousand dollars and two eleven room houses at six thousand each for caretakers. His house overlooked a regulation polo field; later he added a second polo field. His investment in Riverside, and the game of polo, enriched the community in many ways.

During the 1920s and 1930s Victoria Avenue improved in appearance and became a scenic tourist attraction edged in giant eucalyptus trees and tall, skinny palm trees. Nevertheless, in the spring of 1924, the Riverside Trust Company began selling their Arlington Heights properties, mostly planted to citrus, as English stockholders began dissolving their company. The *Riverside Daily Press* printed an editorial approving such action stating "individual owners would live on the land and develop citrus groves that were better managed than a big corporation."

As the Riverside Trust Company continued to sell their properties, new owners became involved in the welfare of Victoria Avenue. Some desired a bridal path down the middle of the center divider strip while other recent arrivals had dozens of other ideas. These suggestions and inquires influenced the creation of several improvement organizations concerned with the maintenance and supervision of Victoria Avenue.

Chapter 12: Family

In 1924, Mary Elizabeth Rumsey and her mother, were living in Los Angeles and the safe and logical disposition of Cornelius's Indian collection surfaced. A number of renown museums were eager to obtain the collection although Mrs. Rumsey wished it to remain in Riverside. She wrote a letter to Riverside's Mayor Samuel Evans and City Council offering the valuable Indian items to the city if it could be housed in the new fireproof City Hall, in a suitable room for public display. "Furthermore, I desire and request that this collection be known as the Cornelius Earle Rumsey Indian Collection." City officials readily agreed to her requests and accepted the more than six hundred articles.

City Hall 1924
J. H. Hall Colletion

There was much correspondence regarding details concerning the collection. Finally, in September Mayor Evans personally supervised the removal of the Indian articles from 6700 Victoria Avenue. Items were carefully packed in trunks and boxes. Ancient and fragile pottery, more than a hundred years old, required special handling along with glass display cabinets and oversized wall hangings.

City Hall 1924
J. H. Hall Colletion

Dedication of the Cornelius Earle Rumsey Indian Museum took place December 12, 1924 in the basement of the new City Hall. Distinguished civic leaders and members of the Rumsey family were present. Mary Elizabeth Rumsey was the guest of honor and she appeared quite fashionable in her ankle length dress and heeled shoes.

Mary Rumsey and her mother spent their later years in Los Angeles at their St. Andrews Place residence. They both lived long lives well into their nineties. The Riverside Woman's Club commemorated the death of each lady, reminding members of their years of volunteer work.

In January 1926, Edward Mortimer Bonnett purchased *Alta Cresta Rancho* and Rumsey's packinghouse. The twenty-six old house and extensive citrus grove sold for one hundred thousand dollars. A second deed for the Pachappa Station Packinghouse was issued upon payment of twenty-five thousand dollars. He sold the packinghouse a year later and

C.E. Rumsey Indian Museum Dedication
J. H. Hall Colletion

invested in a downtown office building on the southeast corner of Eighth (University) and Orange Streets that became known as the Bonnett Building.

Edward Bonnett took out an eight thousand dollar building permit in 1927 to modernize and update the aging Rumsey house. The remodeling obliterated any trace of Victorian design and completely changed the appearance of the landmark house. Regardless of major changes to the notable property, it retained its notable address - 6700 Victoria Avenue.

During the ensuing years, members of the Bonnett and Marvin families became active, productive citizens of Riverside. They served on the City Council, became active members on the Board of Education, YMCA and YWCA directors, and faithful members of the Calvary Presbyterian

Church. The Bonnett families were influential in business transactions and often set the tone for elite social activities.

In the late 1960s, Riverside's Cultural Heritage Board began to list local historic landmarks in order to identify, preserve, and protect city features and sites. Victoria Avenue was selected as Landmark Number 8 due to its age and variety of trees and shrubbery lining the seven mile long road. The Roosevelt Palm, earlier known as the Queen Victoria Palm, was declared Riverside Landmark Number 64. In later years, Victoria Avenue was listed in the National Register of Historic Places.

Postcard of Victoria Avenue
J. H. Hall Collection

Descendants of Edward and Lucy Bonnett occupied the Rumsey house for more than eighty years. Their sons operated the *Alta Cresta Rancho* enterprise until the 1970's when Riverside's citrus industry began to decline. Considerable acreage surrounding the Rumsey house was then developed into a housing development of some sixty units known as *The Trees*.

When other multi-housing projects along Victoria Avenue were proposed, the City of Riverside adopted a greenbelt ordinance to prevent the disorderly development along the historic street, and certain nearby areas. The Victoria zoning proposition, passed by voters in 1987, stated "individuals many construct one single family dwelling on a lot not less than five acres."

Subsequently

The beautification of the Arlington Heights area by Cornelius Rumsey has become evident with the passage of time. The Victoria Avenue trees and vegetation flourish due in part to his early financial support and his many endeavors to beautify the area.

In 1990 Victoria Avenue Forever organized to preserve, restore, and beautify Victoria Avenue. Members have successfully improved and maintained the area much as Cornelius Rumsey did during his pleasurable retirement years.

Family members have occupied the Rumsey House for more than a hundred years and today a remote relative continues to reside there. The Roosevelt Palm Tree and the Rumsey Palm Tree continue to live and stand tall where they were transplanted more than a hundred years ago.

Acknowledgments

I wish to thank Cynthia Stevens, a Rumsey ancestor and the family genealogist, for reading my 2015 manuscript and helping me keep names and relationships in order. I also thank Brad Sackett, who now owns the Rumsey house, for sharing important information and the use of early photographs.

Dr. Archie Shamel, who worked for the US Department of Agriculture, wrote a series of articles that appeared in the Riverside Daily Press, during the 1930s reflecting on Cornelius Rumsey's foresight in the beautification of Victoria Avenue. His articles were very informative.

My thanks to Robin Hanks for encouraging me to have the Rumsey story published and for her remarkable expertise in making it happen.

About the Author

Joan Herrick Hall, is a fourth generation resident of Riverside, California. Her interest in local history began in the early 1960s when she became a Riverside Municipal Museum volunteer.

She has served as chairman of the Riverside Museum Associates, Riverside Cultural Heritage Board, and the Municipal Museum Board. She is the author of various publications including: *Know Your City* (1977), *The Victoria Club 1903-1978* (1978), *A Citrus Legacy* (1992), *Through The Doors of The Mission Inn Vol. 1* (1996), *Vol. 2* (2000), *Cottages, Colonials, and Community Places of Riverside, California* (2003), *Adobes, Bungalows, and Mansions of Riverside Revisited* (2005), *Pursuing Eden* (2008), *Riverside's Invisible Past* (2010) and *Riverside's One & Only Buffalo Heart* (2014).

References

I have eliminated footnotes and endnotes due to the modification of many available sources of reference information. I derived most pertinent facts from a variety of national newspaper articles and obituaries that were a great source of information. Death notices helped me to identify many relationships throughout the generations of large families, many with identical names.

The *Riverside Daily Press* printed numerous articles written by Archie Shamel during the 1930s complimenting Cornelius Rumsey for his beautification of Victoria Avenue. In the May 28, 1936 edition of the *Press*, the Physiologist with the United States Bureau of Plant Industry, named and located a great number of trees planted by Cornelius Rumsey. Shamel gave Rumsey much credit for the condition of Victoria Avenue and the surrounding area.

Several early issues of the *Reports of the Riverside Museum Associates* contained informative articles concerning the Rumseys.

Reference Notes:

Riverside Press & Horticulturist: October 9, 1892, Philpot property.

Riverside Daily Press: May 12, 1892 - Riverside High School accredited for college entrance.

Riverside Daily Press May 25, 1898 - Franchise granted to Frank Miller for electric railroad from Main Street to Victoria Avenue to Van Buren Avenue to Magnolia Avenue.

Philadelphia Inquirer: March 20 , 1899. - A.S. Marvin known as Edison of manufacturing.

Jersey Journal, New Jersey: June 8, 1968 - Antonio Nicolo worked for Marvin Safe Company and decorated safe doors with landscape and nautical scenes.

Riverside Press & Horticulturist: February 8, 1901 - Part of Myrtle Street renamed Victoria Avenue due to Rumsey.

Riverside Daily Press: May 29, 1901 - Joseph, Mission Inn parrot.

Riverside Press & Horticulturist: November 29. 1901 - Rumsey's salary, $10,000.

Riverside Daily Press: May 3, 1903 - Rumsey's idea to dedicate to Queen Victoria - Roosevelt Palm tree at head of Victoria Avenue.

Riverside Daily Press: May 28, 1936 - Archie Shamel article

Riverside Daily Press: May 28, 1936 - Rumsey missing diamond from ring after tree planting.

Riverside Daily Press: March 9, 1905 - Oranges from Parent Navel Tree in Mission Inn garden are harvested and sent to President Theodore Roosevelt.

Riverside Daily Press: February 26, 1906 - Korean labor and articles by Dr. Vincent Moses concerning Ahn Chang Ho.

Inland Empire Magazine: September 1981 - Murder on Victoria Avenue (1907) by Joan Hall.

Riverside Daily Press: February 18, 1937 - Series of articles by Archie Shamel on Victoria Avenue and Cornelius Rumsey's contributions.

Riverside Daily Press: December 15, 1943 - Dr. J. H. Kellogg obituary.

Press-Enterprise: December 5, 2016.

Books:

Through The Doors of the Mission Inn, Volume One by Joan Hall.

A Colony For California by Tom Patterson - 1971

History of Riverside City and County by John R. Gabbert - 1933

Riverside Community Book by Arthur Paul - 1954

History of Riverside County by Elmer W. Holmes - 1912

History of San Bernardino and Riverside Counties by Brown & Boyd - 1922.

Newspapers:

Riverside Daily Press

Riverside Independent Enterprise

Riverside Press & Horticulturist

New York Evening Post

New York Tribune

Philadelphia Enquirer

Other Sources:

California Citrograph September 1936

GenealogyBank.com

Inland Empire Magazine September 1981

The Riverside and Arlington   Electric Railway; Interurban Magazine 1962

Riverside City and County Directories

Riverside Museum Associates Report February 1966

Riverside Public Library

Riverside Metropolitan Museum Archives

Photographs:

Joan Hall Collection

Riverside Metropolitan Museum

Sunset Magazines 1900s

Index

94997243R00059

Made in the USA
Columbia, SC
03 May 2018